Google Home

Complete Manual Book to Master Your Smart Assistant. Unofficial Guide for Beginners

By Nicholas Brown

Copyright©2017 Nicholas Brown
All Rights Reserved

Copyright © 2017 by Nicholas Brown

All rights reserved. No part of this publication may be reproduced, distributed, or transmitted in any form or by any means, including photocopying, recording, or other electronic or mechanical methods, without the prior written permission of the author, except in the case of brief quotations embodied in critical reviews and certain other noncommercial uses permitted by copyright law.

Table of Contents

Introduction	5
Chapter 1- Getting Started with Google Home	6
Chapter 2- How to Use Google Home	12
Chapter 3- Playing TV Movies and Shows with Google Home	19
Chapter 4- Playing Audio on Speakers	31
Chapter 5- Smart Lights with Google Home	36
Chapter 6- Google Home and Thermostat	46
Chapter 7- Google Home and WeMo	52
Chapter 8- Tips and Tricks	60
Conclusion	68

Disclaimer

While all attempts have been made to verify the information provided in this book, the author does assume any responsibility for errors, omissions, or contrary interpretations of the subject matter contained within. The information provided in this book is for educational and entertainment purposes only. The reader is responsible for his or her own actions and the author does not accept any responsibilities for any liabilities or damages, real or perceived, resulting from the use of this information.

The trademarks that are used are without any consent, and the publication of the trademark is without permission or backing by the trademark owner. All trademarks and brands within this book are for clarifying purposes only and are the owned by the owners themselves, not affiliated with this document.

Introduction

With the advancement in technology, most people from all over the world are now beginning to use the technology of voice recognition. With Google Home, one can use voice commands only so as to do a number of tasks while at home. A good example of such a task is control of the lighting system of a house. Google Home can help you to accomplish this task without having to lift a finger. This book guides you on how to use Google Home. You will learn how to set it up and use it to do your tasks. Enjoy reading!

Chapter 1- Getting Started with Google Home

What is Google Home?

This is a smart speaker which was developed by Google and is powered by the Google Assistant. The speaker is voice-activated. This device can be used for the purpose of automating your home so that you can do most tasks without being very involved physically. With Google Home, you can control your smart home devices such as Philips Hue, Nest Thermostat, and others.

Unlike other devices such as the Android voice assistant, you can do much with Google Home without the need of pulling out your phone. This is just a standalone device which you are able to place on a desk or anywhere else and use it at any time that you need at your convenience.

Setting up Google Home

The process of setting up Google Home will only take you a few minutes. After plugging in the device, it will boot up automatically and then you will have to download and install the Google Home app on your phone. Note that this app comes with versions for both Android and iOS.

Begin by downloading this app from the Google Pay Store into your phone. Once this is completed, plug the power adapter into the power outlet, and then connect the other end of this to the speaker. This should be done on the input which is located on the bottom of your speaker. You will see Google Home begin to boot up and an array of lights will be shown.

Next, on your smart phone, open your Home app, then tap on the "*DEVICES*" icon which is located on top-right corner of the screen. Find the Google Home entry from the "*DEVICES*" screen, and then tap on "*SET UP,*" then on "*CONTINUE.*"

The smart phone will now be switched to the temporary Wi-Fi which is on the Google Home. Once the connection has been established, it will be good for you to ensure that you have been connected to the right Google Home device. You just have to press the "Play Test Sound" button. If a voice is heard from the Google Home, just press "I heard it."

The new device will then be named. There are multiple room options from which you can choose, and this is based on where you need to keep your device. In case your room is not in the list, or if you need to use a different one, just tap on the "Other." You will then be given a chance to type in the name for the device, so just do so, and then tap on "Continue."

You will then be in your next step, which is connecting your Google Home to the Wi-Fi network. Select the type of network which you need to establish a connection to, and then type in the corresponding password.

It is possible for you to permit the app so that it can retrieve the password automatically instead of having to type it. This can be enabled from your Smartphone. For you to use the network password which was saved, just tap on "OK." After connection to the Wi-Fi network has been established, just tap on "Continue."

The device will then begin to download and install the updates automatically. Once the update has been completed, tap on the "Sign in" button so that the Google account can be added to the Google Home. On your next screen, choose the Google account which you need, and then tap on the "Continue" button so as to proceed.

Google Home will prove to be very helpful to you only if it is aware of your personal information such as flights and calendar events. If you need to grant it access to such information, just tap on "Allow."

If you need to get highly accurate information regarding the weather or traffic as well as local business information, you should provide your address. Once you have provided this address, just tap on the button for "Set location."

In the next step, you will be given the option of whether to receive the email notifications or not regarding new apps, features, offers, and others. If you want to receive notifications, just toggle the button so that you turn it on, and then tap on "Continue."

At the moment, Google Home can be integrated with only a number of music services including YouTube Music, Google Play Music, Pandora, and Spotify. Identify the music service which you need to set as the default, tap on it, and then tap on "Continue."

You will then have completed the setup process.

You can then press the "Continue" button, and you will be provided with a guide on how to use Google Home. You will be provided with some of the voice commands which you can use together with Google Home. If you need to continue reading the tutorial, just tap on "Continue." If you don't need to do so, just press "Skip."

Chapter 2- How to Use Google Home

Now that you have setup your Google Home, the next step should be to use it, which most probably, you don't know how to. Let us discuss some of the ways that you can exercise control over your device:

Adjusting Volume on Google Home

The top panel of Google Home is a touch pad. It can be used for playing music, pausing music, or to increase and decrease the volume.

In case you are near Google Home and you need to adjust the volume, press a finger down on the top panel, and then move it in the clockwise direction so as to increase the direction. If you need to decrease the volume, then your finger should be moved in the counter clockwise direction.

Also, you can use a voice command so as to adjust the volume. The following are some of the commands which can help you do this:

"Hey Google, increase volume."

"Hey Google, increase volume to maximum."

The first command given above will just increase the volume of Google Home, but the second one will increase the volume to the maximum. Other than increasing the volume, you may also need to decrease the volume by the use of voice commands. This can be done by issuing the following commands:

"Hey Google, decrease volume."

"Hey Google, decrease volume to minimum."

The first command given above will simply decrease the volume, while the second one will decrease the volume to the minimum.

Muting Google Home

Sometimes, you may not want your Google Home to produce any noise or sound, calling for you to mute it, which is a very easy process. A microphone button will be available at the back of your device and towards the top.

Just press that button, and Google Home will state "microphone off." In this state, your Google Home is unable to play any music, respond to any queries, or do anything else until the time you have unmated it. If you need to unmated this device, just press the button once, and you will hear the sound "microphone on" from the device.

Also, it is possible for you to mute this device by use of a voice command, but for you to unmate it; you will have to tap on the microphone button at its back. The command for muting this device should be as follows:

"Hey Google, mute your microphone."

The command will just mute your device.

Rebooting Google Home

Sometimes, this device may fail to work correctly. In such a situation, you may have to reboot it so that everything can be reset. To do this, launch the Google app on your smart phone, and press the "Devices" button which is located on the top-right corner of the screen. Find the Google Home device, and then press the overflow menu button. Select "Reboot." A prompt will appear asking you whether to reboot your device. Just press the "OK," and your device will be rebooted.

Factory Resetting Google Home

Note that this is the process of clearing all the data which is on your Google Home device. It is impossible for you to undo the process. Note that it is impossible for you to use voice or the Home app so as to factory reset the Google Home device. However, this process can be easily done from the device itself as explained below:

Locate the microphone button which is on the back of your device. Tap and then hold this button down for about 15 seconds. The Google Assistant will confirm to you that it is resetting the device, and a series of lights will be seen filling up the circle which is on your top of the device. Once you see this circle fill up, then your device will have been reset to its default settings.

Enabling the Guest Mode

In some cases, you may be in a social gathering, and you need to grant others access to the Google Home device. This is a good way of keeping your password safe, but the guests will be granted access to the device, provided they are in the same room with the device.

The following are the necessary steps for you to enable the Guest Mode: Launch the Google Home app on your smart phone and then tap on the "Devices" button which is located on the top-right corner of the screen.

Identify the Home Device, and tap on the overflow menu button, which are the three vertical dots, and select "Settings." Scroll downwards, and then choose "Guest Mode." Toggle this button so as to turn on the Guest Mode. You will see a four digit pin generated, and this should be used in your device. This is the pin which you should use for sharing the device with your guests.

After that, it will be easy for you to cast the device as a guest. You just have to launch any of the Google Cast-enabled devices and then tap on "cast icon." You can then tap on the nearby device, and then follow through the prompts presented to you, and the connection will be established. In case you experience a problem with the audio pairing, just ask the host for this pin with 4 digits. This pin can also be found from the "Devices" screen of the Google Home app. With that, you will be in a position to use your friend's Google Home device even though you may not be using the same Wi-Fi network.

Chapter 3- Playing TV Movies and Shows with Google Home

For you to play your TV movies and shows on Google Home, you should first begin by linking the TV to the Google Home app. This can be done by following the sequence of steps given below:

1. Begin by setting up the Google Home Device.

2. Launch the Google Home app on your smart phone.

3. From top left corner of your Home screen, tap on "Menu."

4. Verify that the Google Account which has been listed is the one which you used when setting up Google Home. For you to switch the accounts, click on the triangle located on the right of your account name.

5. Make sure that the supported devices have been set up and are on a similar Wi-Fi network with Google Home.

6. Tap on "More settings> TVs and Speakers." A list with all the linked devices will be presented to you.

7. If you need to link a new Chromecast or a TV with the Chromecast built-in, just tap on the plus sign located at bottom right corner of your screen.

8. The Google Home app should search for the voice-supported TVs on the same Wi-Fi network as Google Home. Note that devices which are not voice-supported may be shown in the list. These cannot be linked to the Google Home currently, but they will be available very soon.

9. To add the device, tap on the checkbox located on the right of your device name. You can choose multiple devices and tap on "Add."

10. All the devices will be shown within the TVs and the speakers section of your Google Home app.

11. In case you get the "Error when linking device" as an error message, you should Factory Data Reset (FDR) the Chromecast device.

Although this is not very necessary at this point, you may need to unlink the device in the future. To do this, you should follow the steps given below:

1. From the top right corner of your Home screen, tap on "Devices."

2. Scroll to the bottom and then tap on "Linked Devices."

3. Tap on the X located next to the device you need to unlink.

In the next step, you have to link the video apps to the Google account. This is because some video apps will require you to do this.

The following are the steps which will help you to accomplish this:

1. Launch your Google Home app from your smart phone.

2. From the top left corner of your Home screen, tap on "Menu."

3. Verify that Google Account which has been listed is the one which was used for setting up the Google Home. If you need to switch the accounts, just click on the triangle located to the right of your account name.

4. Ensure that the supported devices have been set up, and that they are on a similar Wi-Fi network with Google Home.

5. Tap on More settings> Videos and photos.

6. Within the section for Videos, scroll so as to find your video app.

7. If the app needs linking, tap on Link >Link account. It is good for you to know that the Google Home will automatically link the main Netflix profile to the Google Home. Linking of secondary profiles isn't supported.

8. Complete the sign in steps.

Again, this is not necessary, but you may need to unlink your video apps. In this case, you can follow the steps given below:

1. Launch the Google Home app from your smartphone.

2. From the top left corner of your Home screen, tap on Menu.

3. Verify that the Google Account which has been listed is the one which you had used for setting up Google Home. For you to switch the accounts, click on the triangle located to the right of your account name.

4. Ensure that the supported devices have been set up and they are on a similar Wi-Fi network with Google Home.

5. Tap on More settings>Videos and photos.

6. Within the section for Videos, scroll so as to identify the video app.

7. Tap on Unlink> Unlink account so as to confirm that you need to unlink your video app account from the Google Account. You won't be able to make use of voice commands so as to play video app's media on Google Home.

The Voice Commands for TV Control

The following are the voice commands which can help you to talk to the Google Assistant on Google Home so as to play TV movies and shows.

If you to play some TV show, or TV series or a movie, begin by saying:

"Ok Google." or

"Hey Google."

This should then be followed by either of the following:

"Watch <The Three Idiots> <on TV>." or

"Watch < The Three Idiots > <on/from Netflix> <on TV>."

"Watch < The Lego Batman Movie > <on Chromecast>." or

"Watch < The Lego Batman Movie > <on/from Netflix> <on Chromecast>."

"Play < The Lego Batman Movie > <on TV>." or

"Play < The Lego Batman Movie > <on/from Netflix> <on TV>."

To play the next episode or the previous one, use the following commands:

"Next episode <on TV>."
"Previous episode <on TV>."

Note that in all of these commands, you should begin by saying, "Ok Google" or "Hey Google," which should then be followed by your command. For you to pause, resume, or stop an episode from playing, use the following command options:

"Pause <on TV>."
"Resume <on TV>."
"Stop <on TV>."

To skip back, say the following voice commands, while not forgetting to start with "Ok Google" or "Hey Google":

"Skip back <time> <on TV>,"

"Rewind <time> <on TV>,"

"Jump back <time> <on TV>."

To turn on captions or subtitles, use the following commands:

"Turn on subtitles,"

"Turn on captions,"

"Subtitles on," "Captions on."

To turn the captions or subtitles off, use the following voice commands:

"Turn off subtitles,"

"Turn off captions,"

"Subtitles off,"

"Captions off."

Note that for those who only have cone voice-supported cast device linked, it is not mandatory for you to say its name in the command. It is possible for you to use the following:

"Ok Google, ...<on TV>." or

"Ok Google, ...<on Chromecast>."

Tips and Tricks

After you begin to play a TV show or a movie by use of your voice such as, "Ok, Google. Watch The Lego Batman Movie on TV," all the next control commands such as pause, next, and others will control your TV. You will not want to continue to specify the TV after the viewing session begins.

If you began playing some TV show or a movie on a TV by casting from the phone or a tablet, you will want to first add the <on TV> and then after doing this once, you will not have to say the <on TV> again.

When a media is playing on the Google Home simultaneously with some remote device, all the control commands will control the Google Home, but not the remote devices.

For you to control the remote device, you should always say the phrase "Ok Google, ... <on device>."If you have stopped playing the content on the Google Home by simply saying the phrase

"Ok Google, stop," and there is a need to start controlling a remote device which is currently playing, one should first add the phrase <on device> to the next command which is made to the remote device.

Example, "Ok Google, next video <on TV>. It is also possible to follow the steps given below so as to control your TV from your Google Home app:

1. Ensure that your mobile device or the tablet has been connected to a similar Wi-Fi as the remote device.

2. Launch your Google Home app from the smart phone.

3. From the top right corner of the app Home screen, just tap on Device settings.

4. Scroll so as to find your device card for Google Home.

5. It is possible for you to pause/resume, stop, as well as control your remote device from device card.

Chapter 4- Playing Audio on Speakers

It is possible for us to play audio on external speakers or a TV by use of Google Home. The first step should be to link the speakers and the TV by use of the Google Home app. Note that the both the speakers and the TV must be voice-enabled. The connection can be done by following the steps given below:

1. Begin by setting up Google Home.

2. Launch your Google Home app.

3. From top left corner of your Home screen, tap on Menu.

4. Verify that Google Account which has been listed is the one which you used for setting up Google Home. For you to switch the accounts, just click on the triangle located to the right of your account name.

5. Ensure that your supported devices have been set up, and they are on a similar Wi-Fi network as Google Home.

6. Tap on More settings> TVs and Speakers. A list of all the linked devices will be presented.

7. To link your new Chromecast Audio or the speakers or the TVs with the Chromecast built-in, just tap on the plus sign located in the bottom right corner of your screen.

8. The Google Home app will then search for the voice-supported speakers and the TVs on a similar Wi-Fi network as Google Home. It is possible for you to see a list of devices which are not voice-supported. Such cannot be linked to Google Home.

9. To add a device, just tap the checkbox located to the right of your device name. Note that it is possible for you to check multiple devices. Press "Add."

10. All your devices will then be shown within the TVs and the speakers section in the Google Home app.

11. In case you get the error message "Error when linking device," you should Factory Data Reset (FDR) the Chromecast Audio device.

Your devices should also be named properly so that there can be a proper playback on the speakers. When naming these devices, ensure that the name can be easily pronounced, and avoid the use of special characters or emojis. The following are the steps which will help you to change the name of the devices:

1. Launch the Google Home app from your smart phone.

2. From the top right corner of your Home screen, just tap on "Devices" so as to see the available Google Home and the Chromecast/Chromecast Audio devices.

3. Scroll so as to find device card for your Google Home or the Chromecast/Chromecast Audio device which you need to rename.

4. From top right corner of your device card, tap on device card menu > Settings> Name. Delete the available name and then type in some new name. Press "SAVE".

To make you aware, to play audio from Google Home, you can use devices such as Chromecast, Chromecast audio, Android TV devices, as well as TVs and speakers which have Chromecast built-in.

Once you have setup your devices, you can use the necessary voice commands so as to exercise over the audio to the speakers and TVs.

10. All your devices will then be shown within the TVs and the speakers section in the Google Home app.

11. In case you get the error message "Error when linking device," you should Factory Data Reset (FDR) the Chromecast Audio device.

Your devices should also be named properly so that there can be a proper playback on the speakers. When naming these devices, ensure that the name can be easily pronounced, and avoid the use of special characters or emojis. The following are the steps which will help you to change the name of the devices:

1. Launch the Google Home app from your smart phone.

2. From the top right corner of your Home screen, just tap on "Devices" so as to see the available Google Home and the Chromecast/Chromecast Audio devices.

3. Scroll so as to find device card for your Google Home or the Chromecast/Chromecast Audio device which you need to rename.

4. From top right corner of your device card, tap on device card menu > Settings> Name. Delete the available name and then type in some new name. Press "SAVE".

To make you aware, to play audio from Google Home, you can use devices such as Chromecast, Chromecast audio, Android TV devices, as well as TVs and speakers which have Chromecast built-in.

Once you have setup your devices, you can use the necessary voice commands so as to exercise over the audio to the speakers and TVs.

The voice command should begin with the following phrase as usual:

Say "Ok Google" or

"Hey Google."

You should then add the following commands, based on what you want to do: To play audio on a particular device by name, use the following commands:

"Play <artist> using <Spotify> on <living room speakers>."

"Pause on <bedroom room TV>."

"Play classical music on <Patio group>."

"Stop <Patio group>."

Note that for those who have linked only a single device, there is no need for you to say its name.

Chapter 5- Smart Lights with Google Home

The Philips Hue is compatible with Google Assistant and Google Home for controlling all the lights in your house, whenever you are in your house, using only the sound of voice. It is possible for you to turn off hallway lights or to dim living room lights hands-free using your Assistant. Are you interested in controlling your lights using any other way? After adding a Google on Hub router to the home, you will be able to invite your guests so as to control lights directly.

Together, the Philips Hue and Google provide you with a simple solution for controlling the lights at your home. To connect the Philips Hue to Google Home and then control it with your voice, follow the steps given below:

1. Begin by launching the Google Home app from your smart phone, and then press the Devices button which is located on the top right corner of the screen.

The Red arrow is pointing to the Devices button, so just tap it.

2. Press the menu button which is located on the upper right corner of the screen.

The red arrow points to the menu button so go ahead and tap it. Choose "Settings" and then tap on the "Home Control."

3. Identify the round plus button which is located on the bottom-right corner of the screen, and then tap on it.

4. Choose "Philips Hue." Note that you will see a list of the devices which are supported, but since we need to connect to the Philips Hue, you have to choose it.

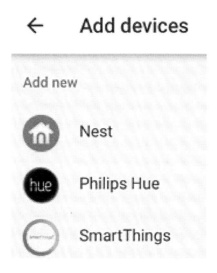

5. On your next screen, tap the "Pair" option located at the bottom, and then tap on the big button which is on the Hue Bridge Hub.

If the pairing was successful, then you will get a message which alerts you of the same. You can then tap on the "Assign

Rooms" option which is located on the bottom right corner of the screen.

You will see the Philips Hue bulbs in the list, and it is possible for you to begin controlling them by the use of voice commands. It will be good for you to group your bulbs into rooms, and your experience will be good. On the top of the screen, tap on the "Rooms" tab.

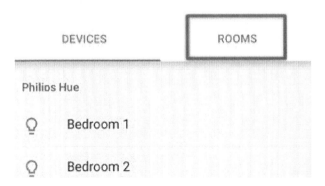

Identify the round plus button at the bottom-right corner of the screen, and then tap on it. You will see a list of rooms presented to you, and you can choose a room from the list. Note that that is the name which you will use to identify your room, and you should add that name in your voice commands to Google Home.

It is also possible for you to scroll downwards, and then click on "Add Custom Room." This will give you the option of giving the room the name which you want; provided that Google Home is able to recognize it once you pronounce it.

After selecting a room, just place checkmarks to the Philips Hue Bulb which is to be associated with the room. Once done, press "Done" located in top-right corner after you have selected the bulbs.

The room will then be shown as part of the list, and it is possible for you to click on the round plus button again so as to add more rooms. Once you are sure that all the rooms which you need to control have been added, you can close the app and then begin to use the voice commands so as to control the lighting system of your house.

Note that the Google Home supports a number of commands which can be used for the purpose of controlling the Philips Hue lighting system. Some of the actions which you can accomplish include turning the lights on and off, setting the percentage for the lights, brightening and dimming the lights as well as changing the color of the lights.

The following are examples of Google Home commands which can be used for accomplishing this:

- "Ok Google, turn on the living room lights."
- "Ok Google, brighten the bedroom lights."
- "Ok Google, dim the office lights."

- "Ok Google, set (dim/brighten) reading light to 70%."

- "Ok Google, turn off all the lights."

You should note that it is impossible for you to activate scenes via Google Home, meaning that if you use a voice command like "Ok Google, turn on Relax scene in the bedroom," it will not work.

Sometimes, you may need to rename a particular room. Note that these are the rooms you added by clicking on the round plus button. This can be done by following the steps given below:

1. From the ROOMS tab, a list of the rooms and the assigned lights will be available.

2. Tap on the room's name which you need to adjust.

3. Tap on the name of the room.

4. Type the new name, and tap on OK >Done.

5. All the lights which have been listed under a new room name will be shown.

Also, you may need to change the lights for a particular room. This can be done by following the sequence of steps given below:

1. From the ROOMS tab, a list of all rooms together with the assigned lights will be given.

2. Tap on the room name on which you would like to do the adjustment.

3. Select the light which you would want to move and tap on Move.

4. Tap the radio button which is next to the room you would want to move this to.

1. To add a room which has not been listed, just scroll down and then tap the "+ CUSTOM ROOM >, then type the room name > OK."

5. Tap on "Done."

6. You will then observe that the light is not now listed in the room which you have moved it from.

If you need to change the color of the light, you can use the following voice command:

"Ok Google, turn <light name> green."

The command will turn your lights to green, and you will see them change their color. You can also specify the percentage by which you need to brighten or dim your lights. The following command can help you achieve this. This will dim your light by 30 percent.

Ok Google, Dim/Brighten <light name> by 30%."

Chapter 6- Google Home and Thermostat

It is possible for you to connect Google Home to your Nest thermostat and then use voice commands so as to control it. To do this, follow the steps given below:

On your smart phone, open the Google Home app and then observe the side menu. A section for Home Control will be available, and this will have things such as the Nest thermostat.

Move to the bottom of this page, and then tap on the round plus button. A list of devices to be added to this will be presented, so you just have to choose "Nest." Google Home will show you what should be done with the skill, and then a prompt for continue will be visible.

You should log into the Nest account from the window which is given as a popup, and if the connection is done, a success message will be presented to you. Google should also be informed of the room in which you have kept the Nest so that the hardware in the app can be better organized. You will then be connected.

Now that the connection is okay, you should go ahead and begin to speak. Google Home will be in a position to respond to the commands which you issue, provided your thermostat is on. The following are some of the commands which will help you to control the temperature of your house. To adjust the temperature, use the following list of commands:

"Ok Google, Make it warmer/cooler,"

"Ok Google, Raise/lower the temp,"

"Ok Google, Raise/lower temp 2 degrees,"

"Ok Google, Set the temperature to 72."

Those commands will help you to adjust the temperature by either raising or lowering it. To switch between the heating and the cooling modes, use the following set of commands:

"Turn on the heat/cooling,"

"Set the thermostat to cooling/heating,"

"Turn thermostat to heat-cool mode."

Those commands will help you to set your Nest thermostat into the mode which you need. If you need to set the mode as well as the temperature, use the commands given below:

"Set the heat to 66."
"Set the air conditioning to 72."

If you need to turn the thermostat off via a voice command, use the one given below:

"Turn off thermostat."

If you need to use the name of the room you have kept the thermos stat in when adjusting the temperature, execute the following command:

"Set the <BedRoom> thermostat to 68."

If you need to know the ambient temperature of your thermostat, use the following voice command, and you will hear it:

"What's the temperature inside?"

To know the temperature your thermostat has been set to, use the following voice command and you will hear it:

"What's the thermostat set to?"

Those are the commands which can help you when you are using your Nest thermostat connected to Google Home. Sometimes, you may need to unlink your thermostat from Google Home. To do this, follow the sequence of steps given below:

To do it from the Google Home app, follow the steps given below:

1. From the DEVICES tab, a list of the rooms and the assigned thermostat(s) will be shown.

2. In top right corner of your screen, tap on "More"> "Manage Accounts."

3. Tap on the account which you would like to unlink.

4. Tap on "Unlink account > Unlink."

5. At the screen's bottom, you will see a confirmation of your unlinked account.

It is also possible for you to unlink your Nest thermostat from the SmartThings or Nest app. This can be achieved by following the steps given below. This can be achieved by following the similar steps which have been used in the above process.

Chapter 7- Google Home and WeMo

WeMo provides you with a simple and easy way to control your home. However, it requires you to use your fingertips. For you to make it easy, you should connect it with Google Home.

The users can use natural speech patterns so as control any WeMo connected devices after the WeMO has been connected to Google Home via Google Assistant.

Do you have a fan which is controlled by WeMo? You only have to link your WeMo to Google Home and then issue the following command so as to turn on the fan:

"Ok Google, turn on the fan."

The above command will turn on the fan. Once you link the WeMo and Google Home, it becomes possible for you to control any electronic device which has a on/off switch. Other gadgets which you will be able to control include the overhead lights, porch lights, and the chandeliers.

Google Home also permits individuals to group the WeMo devices so that you control the entire room and or scenarios by the use of a single statement. Consider the example command given below:

"Ok Google, turn on the living room."

Once you say the above voice command, it is possible for the overhead lights, table lamps, as well as the window AC unit to be turned on at a similar time.

To enable this, the users have to be running Wemo firmware of version 10885 or a higher version for both the iOS and Android, and these are currently available.

Wemo Mini Smart Plug is a good example of a WeMo device. It allows you to control your electronic devices from a phone or tablet. This Smart Plug makes use of an existing home Wi-Fi network so as to provide a wireless control of your lamps, fans, heaters, and more, and you will not be required to have a subscription or a hub.

You simply have to plug your Wemo Mini Smart Plug into an electrical outlet, plug the device into a Smart Plug, and then control the device by use of your free Wemo app. With this, it will be possible for you to control your lights as well as other appliances remotely from any part of the world.

The device will allow you to set schedules on how to put devices such as your lights on and then have lights in your smart home. By use of the free Wemo app, it becomes possible for you to schedule your fan to turn on during noon, or to synchronize your lamp with sunset so that you don't come home to a dark house.

The WeMo Light Switch is also another WeMo device which lets you turn your lights on and off from any place, either from the house, the backyard, or the other side of the world. It replaces the standard light switch which you are using in your home, and it can be controlled remotely by use of an Android smartphone or a tablet, iPad, iPhone, or iPod touch.

It will work well with the existing Wi-Fi network from any place your smartphone or a tablet has an Internet connection.

IFTTT stands for "If This Then That." It is simply an online service to which smart devices can establish a connection to, and then it facilitates communication between these devices. There are hundreds of devices which can be connected to the IFTTT.

It is easy for you to get these systems communicating. You have to pick what will be used as a trigger. This will work in the same way that Google Home works with the Google Assistant. Once you have everything that you need up and running, it will be time for you to tell it what to do via the voice commands. This is very easy:

- Open "Settings" from the WeMo app.

- Find the entry which says that "Connect to IFTTT," and then tap it.

- Tap the green button which says "Connect."

You can then choose the type of WeMo device which you need to connect to, and then log into the IFTTT page which will be opened. Note that after doing that, you will have connected your WeMo device to the IFTTT, and it is possible for you to make an applet. The same steps should then be repeated for all the WeMo devices which you need to connect. This is because these devices are all located in different channels.

Let us demonstrate how we can create an applet which can help Google to turn the lights on and off by use of the WeMo Light Switch. Tap on the + symbol, sign into the IFTTT app, and then create a new applet. You should then create a trigger. All IFTTT applets expect to have a trigger which will be used for telling it when to run, and because we are to use Google Home, our trigger will be the Google Assistant.

This can be found on the applets page, and you can instruct it to make use of some simple phrase for triggering and action. We will use this for turning off the lights.

You should then type in the words which you need to say whenever you want your switch to be turned off. There are different ways that you can set this, but it is good to use the best one for you who will make it look natural.

After you are done with that, you can go ahead and then type what you want it to say once it has recognized your command and it is turning off the switch. Tap on the checkmark so that the trigger can be saved, and then set the action which you will need to happen.

Note that the IFTTT app can allows you to edit your applet. Inthe case of the action, choose "WeMo Light Switch channel.". You can then tap on the "Turn Off" button. You can then choose the switch which will be turned off. Once you are done, tap on the checkmark and select "Finish" and then "Save."

In my case, I will say "OK Google. Turn off the Living Room lights," while Google Home will tell me "OK. I am turning off the Living Room lights" and the lights will go off. You must say the phrase which you specified, and then Google Home will respond with its corresponding phrase.

Note that in this applet, we chose Turn Off. The process of creating an applet for turning on the lights is the same, only that you should choose Turn On as the action.

Chapter 8- Tips and Tricks

Most people see Google Home as just a speaker, but there is much you can do with it. The following are the best tips and tricks which can help you master this speaker.

Always use the wake word

There are two wake words which can be used in Google Home, "Hey Google" and "Ok Google." There is no way to change these two. Every time you need to use Google Home, you have to say one of the two phrases.

Adjust settings and preferences

Open the Google Home app, then slide out the menu drawer from the left side of your screen, and then tap on More Settings.

You may choose to tap on your name, and then add a Home address for the specified traffic and weather reports. It is also possible for you to set a nickname which you will be using

Rename Google Home

Under settings, open Name, and then you can rename Google Home the way that you like.

Make use of the Google Ecosystem

It is good for you to use other products from Google so as to improve your experience. It has been designed so that it can be integrated with devices such as Google Keep and Google Calendar.

This will help you achieve a lot, including managing your shopping list by the use of voice commands.

Control Google Home via Touch

Rather than the use of voice, it is possible for you to control Google Home via touch. Tap the top of your speaker once so as to awaken Google Home or so as to pause and play some broadcast. It is possible for you to slide the finger along the centered circle located at the top so as to change the volume.

Use it as Google.com

Google Home can be used as an assistant and for setting appointments, and it can double as a search engine. It is possible for you to ask the follow-up questions. The Google Assistant will remember the subject or topic in the string of questions. Use Google Home is to learn the capital city of a particular country, the age of your president, and for conversion of ounces to cups.

Check your activity

Under More Settings, scroll to the bottom and then tap on the My Activity option. You will see a website opened, together with everything that Google Home (and the Assistant on the phone) has recorded. This can be sorted by time and date, play back what Home heard, also get details, as well as delete them.

Cast your Photos to the TV

Google Home can control Google Photos, which is the cloud photo storage service for Google. Link up your account in the Google Home app under the settings, then say the phrase "Okay Google, show me photos of my son on TV." This service is capable of tagging and recognizing people, places. And things and it can serve you with anything that you ask for.

Manage your family shopping list

Google Cast has been built directly into the Chrome browser. Once you click on the cast button in the corner of the Chrome browser, it is possible for you to look for the Home device, choose it, and then cast an audio from the computer to Google Home.

Find a misplaced phone

Can't find your phone? You can use Google Home to locate the device. You only have to link the device with a service named IFTTT. With this, it will be possible for you to call your phone number once you say the phrase "Okay Google, find my phone."

Get to know about your day

Once you asks Google Home "tell me about my day," it can give you an audio report about your calendar, the morning traffic commute, weather, and other reminders. The report can also be customized so as to exclude some things such as the weather. The end result for this will be a news briefing. However, for you to achieve any of these, you must connect services such as Google Calendar by use of settings in the Google Home app.

Funny Questions

The following are some of the funny questions for Google Home:

1. What's your name?

Once you talk to the Google Assistant for the first time, you should be determined to know the name of the Google Assistant. It will answer, "Did I forget to introduce myself? I'm your Google Assistant. Hi!" It may also say, "I'm your Google Assistant." If you follow this up with some name-related question (such as "What's your last name?" the voice assistant will not say much. It will simply answer, "My last name is Assistant. I'm your Google Assistant."

2. How old are you?

There are many answers to this question such as "I launched in 2017. So I'm still new." In some other cases, you may get a long explanation. If you ask it, "Have you met John and Hillary?" the Google Assistant will answer, "I'm not sure I have."

3. Are you human?

You will get the answer "I like connecting with people" Or "I'm really personable."

Get to know about your day

Once you asks Google Home "tell me about my day," it can give you an audio report about your calendar, the morning traffic commute, weather, and other reminders. The report can also be customized so as to exclude some things such as the weather. The end result for this will be a news briefing. However, for you to achieve any of these, you must connect services such as Google Calendar by use of settings in the Google Home app.

Funny Questions

The following are some of the funny questions for Google Home:

1. What's your name?

Once you talk to the Google Assistant for the first time, you should be determined to know the name of the Google Assistant. It will answer, "Did I forget to introduce myself? I'm your Google Assistant. Hi!" It may also say, "I'm your Google Assistant." If you follow this up with some name-related question (such as "What's your last name?" the voice assistant will not say much. It will simply answer, "My last name is Assistant. I'm your Google Assistant."

2. How old are you?

There are many answers to this question such as "I launched in 2017. So I'm still new." In some other cases, you may get a long explanation. If you ask it, "Have you met John and Hillary?" the Google Assistant will answer, "I'm not sure I have."

3. Are you human?

You will get the answer "I like connecting with people" Or "I'm really personable."

4. Do you have hair?

You can ask this question, and the response will be "I don't have hair." If you keep on asking the Google Assistant further questions, it will give you the few cuts it is interested in!

5. Where do you live?

Google Home will respond humorously to this question. An example of a response to this might be "I'm stuck inside a device!! Help! Just kidding. I like it in here." You can choose to ask a further question such as "Do you live in the sky," and you will get a humorous response to the question.

6. Can you drive?

This question will be answered like, "I do like to look at cool cars." If you press on by asking it other questions, you will hear the response "Let's just say I'm waiting for Google's self-driving car."

Conclusion

We have come to the end of this guide. Google Home is a good device which can help you to automate most of the tasks that you do in your house. Due to its low cost, most people have turned to using it rather than the Amazon Echo Dot. The Google Home device works in conjunction with the Google Home app, which is installed into a mobile device. The app comes with versions for both iOS and Android operating systems. Google Home can be used for accomplishing tasks such as controlling the lighting system of a house, controlling a Nest Thermostat, and others. All of these tasks can be accomplished by the use of voice commands only and without having to lift a finger.

Made in the USA
San Bernardino, CA
04 June 2018